Y0-BOY-969

fine

811.54
M344f

fine

—

Stefanie Marlis

LIBRARY ST. MARY'S COLLEGE

WITHDRAWN

Apogee Press
Berkeley · California
2000

gift 8/07

for the dogs

The author is grateful to the editors of the following journals in which some of the poems in this book were first published:

Arshile: "behold," "besot," "cahoots," "cajole," "chance," "chatoyant," "gist," "platoon," "susurrus," "utopia," "Lois with the long Polish name," "peace coming on," "dear anne"
Five Fingers Review: "technique," "welter," "rotary"
Fourteen Hills: "ripple," "vent," "snack," "queue," "sfumato," "muscle"
Tundra: "wont"
Volt: "spare coming on"
ZYZZYVA: "imbroglio"

Book design by Philip Krayna Design, Berkeley CA.

Cover image ©2000 by Sharrie Brooks.

©2000 by Stefanie Marlis.

ISBN 0-96699-374-8. Library of Congress Catalog Card Number 99-098077.

Published by Apogee Press, Post Office Box 8177, Berkeley CA, 94707-8177.

Table of Contents

pavilion : 11

peace   coming on : 12

cahoots : 13

cajole : 14

waft : 15

Lois   with the long Polish name : 16

behold : 17

fret : 18

ripple : 19

umbrage : 20

ranch   coming on : 21

chance : 22

chatoyant : 23

sobriquet : 24

coy : 25

imbroglio : 26

wont : 27

dear   Anne : 28

jejune : 29

occur : 30

snack : 31

garble : 32

tumbrel : 33

spare   gave in : 34

turn : 35

besot : 36

creek : 37

platoon : 38

rotary : 39

valentine   held up : 40

shop : 41

muscle : 42

queue : 43

solstice   ever rides : 44

gist : 45

sfumato : 46

twist : 47

susurrus : 48

aver : 49

étui : 50

splendid   this way : 51

utopia : 52

interruptions   finally : 53

elide : 54

etymon : 55

Easter   looking into : 56

green mansions   turned to : 57

shambles : 58

shape : 59

escape : 60

rescue : 61

tempering : 62

disarrangement   nosing closer : 64

vent : 65

thwart : 66

fine : 67

top : 68

noise : 69

neuston : 70

pining   requires : 71

pavilion—an ornate tent, from the Latin *papilio*, butterfly
—we talk about change coming slowly (me-ta-mor-pho-sis),
but, to tell the truth, nothing does. Half the caterpillar's cells
undefined: stunning orange wings fanning blue fire. We talk
about making room in the heart, ropes clanging against the
center pole; all at once, we do, or don't.

peace   coming on

Every evening, a ghost bends down to pick up a stone

(bedtime kiss   the pigment green

there   look!   a rabbit

fuzzy arrow

across a field   soft

Frailty

we call it twilight, an italic moon

stenciled above the marsh

And sometimes now the heart, unmoored, comes to know anew

the shore

progressing

lone   lonely   lovely

cahoots—questionable collaboration, from the French *cahute,* cabin—her left hand opening jars, buttoning flies, making the bed, and skating across the keyboard, all sans the injured partner with its trio of dislocated bones. All sorts of abilities surface at times like this, there being, it seems, as much good luck in accidents as bad luck, the two bunkmates in some cabin in the sky.

cajole—to urge with gentle and repeated appeals; to coax, from the Old French *cajole*, birdcage—there are the daily nudges to loose body and soul; an accident insists: an injured hand lies on the seat, a separate creature. Shortly after the cast comes off, she's reveling in convalescence, a fresher spirit than before the crash, uncaged, songbird slipping into the blue.

waft—to float easily and gently, as on the air, from the Dutch *wachten*, to guard—he attributes his easy-goingness to an easy life. "But," she says, "your family lost everything in the holocaust, your father died when you were sixteen, and your wife committed suicide." "Oh, yeah," he says— a featherweight man of eighty-four—"I never looked at it like that."

Lois   with the long Polish name

there's only this is   the bells
in the midst of each breath

a folding chair

in rising waters

A man walks into a store
smelling like cigars, thinking in yellow and white

this is what Lois said (Lois
who is never lost);

it's possible to have a faith so sure,
to feel as if you know why

no Comice pears

and the man walks in

O!

(god written in fancy script—the skunk's plush tail)

everything arriving as it does

(see-through;

the line casting forwards and backwards at once)

open house eternally

behold—to observe, look at, see, from the Old English *behalden*, to keep—only after he'd gotten dressed, in the pale light of the laundry room, did he discover them. When his girlfriend came in he was down on his knees "quietly" vacuuming the crawling overalls. She'd watched the ants all week; no two ever passed without touching. There was a lot he kept to himself.

fret—to cause to be uneasy, vex, from the Old English, *fretan*, to devour—when, on an immaculately kept lawn, green as a lime, a skunk caught in a metal trap, a few feet from a pinkish fountain, frantically seeks to free itself, someone might pass by, puzzling over the creature's and the captor's struggle, not knowing which futility eats away at us most.

ripple—to display little undulations on the surface, probably from the Norwegian *riple*, to scratch—moon tugging at the surface of the word moon, you offer your neck; I bite it there, where it will most show. Love o'clock, my little waves hastened by your scratching. Why do we try to understand things we'll never understand? We don't understand this either.

umbrage—offense, resentment, from the Latin *umbra*, shadow—things don't work mostly because they don't work the way we expect them to. Here, the horizon leaks orange and red while the moon sits farther up, deaf and blind. Like it or not, light and shade, piano keys, everywhere. Below, there's a town just waking up.

ranch   coming on

       nothing's being said

walking next to one another
                 jumping brooks
                              one watches out for the other
Coming across:
             the carcass of a baby deer
                     a trio of pink mushrooms
                          a forty-mile view

the clouds gather   so do the cows

one quarters an apple
             daylight silently dwindling
                   offering a slice

chance—the unpredictable element in happenings,
from the Latin *cadere*, befall—he drove his girlfriend across
the churning river and into swampy Louisiana in a rented
Neon, pointing out Daquari World, a place where he used to
work. And she pictured him there, short and sexy, whipping
up party-colored drinks for whoever walked in the door.
The wonder: what we fall for.

chatoyant—having a changeable luster, from the French *chatoyer*, to shimmer like cats' eyes—nothing had changed; addicted to possibility, the boyfriend would scurry from one venture to the next, a universe of green meadows. "I should get a dog suit with a zipper," he teased, still wanting the unending love his girlfriends gave their pets, such love his only constant desire.

sobriquet—an affectionate or humorous nickname from the Old French *soubriquet*, to chuck under the chin—bamboo periscopes, capsized lilies: when the real estate appraiser calls we joke about the weather with the camaraderie of a people under siege; the enemy: El Niño! Once again, I'm surprised by how much I can like a stranger and chin-chuck the dog.

COY—artfully or affectedly shy or reserved, from the Old French *coi*, quiet—some half dozen surf the solitude of the Pacific; others, naked too, tuck themselves in around private rocks; most, not modest in the sun, sunbathing, just quiet. Some under umbrellas highlight novels. One nude trots across the sea-blue backdrop bearing a pyramid of green grapes.

imbroglio—a difficult situation, from the Old Italian *imbrogliare*, to tangle—at William Faulkner's house, he suggested they get a better doormat. "All these little stones," he said, "damaging the floors." He has many talents, but he can't keep things straight, can't manage rent. Knows a plethora of things, like that rats eat lead because it tastes sweet. So does he.

wont—to be in the habit of doing something, from the
Middle English *won*, to dwell or abide—when, during lunch
at Duff's Tavern, the younger son went over to the table
of a man who'd cheated the family, the mother looked on,
unperturbed. She had ingrained in her children a belief in
forgiveness, her boy standing there chatting like a squirrel
at home on power lines.

dear   Anne

she calls her seizures glitches

dented spoon   spent fuse

what can one know (how high the moon?) when into any breath
a hole might seep

unknowing is better, she says,

oils

the soul,

keeps we living full

of living

jejune—not interesting, dull, from the Latin *ieiunnus*, meager, dry—every now and then, someone in Bible study worries about God's gender. "He/She maketh me lie down in green pastures," they insist. How unimaginative, he thinks. Seven years since his wife's chemo and her doctor just found a small, gritty-feeling lymph node. "Our logic," he declares, "just doesn't apply upstairs."

occur—to take place, to come about, from the Latin *occurrere* *ob* + *currere*, to run—some chalk it up to vibration, an imitation of the hummingbird's hover, a fence grazed by a cloven hoof. Whatever makes electrons wobble or a deer skittish makes those who can't help but notice one another ready to run, though it's unclear in which direction.

snack—a small or hurried meal, variation of the Middle English *snacchen*, snap—the sensation pops up like a squirrel scurrying out of a hole in a tree. They'd eaten lightly: the meal, in teasing one appetite, triggered another. One lay her body face down on the water, and the other's snapped awake. Hungry for another world, the two of them gathering little love nuts, kisses, love bites.

garble—to mix up or distort, from the Middle English *garbelen*, to remove refuse from spices—at times, no one talks directly into the mouthpiece. Mittened cholla, psychedelic snapdragon, all the desert birds for blocks flock to the garden hotel; they sound mixed up too: a birdsong stew. Confusion, the spice of love-song, everyone trying to sort what's meant from what's said.

tumbrel—a two-wheeled cart that can be tilted to dump a load, from the Old French *tomber*, to let fall—a figure in silhouette wheels a cart from the field toward the heart; whenever we have something that makes us happy, we doubt it. The fear of its being not right keeps it from being right whether it could be or not. Some happiness the figure lets fall like a cartful of melons.

spare   gave in

      after the fifth rainbow

             gave in to beauty:

                          trite   bright   ageless

an unexpected early rain

             where a week ago the dog flew at dragonflies

        seed pods crackling alongside the trail

            those blue-eyed needles   aloft

          —this morning!   the heart   cracking

(spare tire)   like rubber   will

turn—to cause to rotate or revolve, from the Greek *tornos*, tool to make circles with—like the lathe he made the man who made the bowl he gave her. Despite herself, she does a wash for him and is soon annoyed by the clanking of his overalls in the dryer. Suddenly, she remembers he likes them air-dried, armor against sparks and shards of metal, and gets up and hangs them out back.

besot—to muddle or stupify, from the Old French *sot,*
foolish—every hour has its problems: at seven, too many
cars on the road; at six, too many parked, the dog's ball
rolling underneath, and its beauties: one hour's pink in the
west, the next, pearly blue. Either way, the streets she runs
are strung with blossoms, and she's thinking only a fool
would choose love over this.

creek—a watercourse smaller than a river, from the
Old Norwegian *kriki*, bend—fallen, hand-sized, heart-shaped
leaves cover the octopi and treasure chests imprinted on the
plastic pool he bought for the dog. Everything's changing;
everything's turning; soon the rains will come, and the dog
won't want to cool off. Soon everything will sail around
the bend.

platoon—a company or group of people, from the Old French *pelote*, ball—she rode through her dream on a bus where everyone was wearing away. Half were wounded, yet many still had a sense of play; one hid his holes beneath a shaggy orange mask. In the morning, she's thrown a curve ball: the first two cars that roll through the silence wave: friends on their way to work.

rotary—turning on an axis; from the Medieval Latin
rotarius, wheel—each rosebud in turn spinning open,
it takes the boy a long time to find all the eggs in the
garden; an animal's face, not the clock's, the hub of every
action, so much so he cannot keep from chasing each
grey darting across a path whether vole or lizard, and
this morning names his new baby duck *Turbo Limon*.

valentine   held up

percolating on the common-hood of all opposites/
                        we discover gender's irrelevance
            the heart catches and is caught

and the little doors you open   floor me,
                                you'd grow breasts for me

            caught cut clubbed crimped coddled (like an egg)
                        cupped cooped (red hen)

            easy to make light of
                        held up to the light,
                                    your kinky heart, so
comely be

shop—to look for something with the intention of acquiring it, from the Old English *sceoppa*, treasure house—he didn't buy anything, not that he didn't have things in mind (low-riding jeans, sandals); it was trust he wanted: to earn it, to have it. He looked for it as always in that treasure house sex, pulled a hunting knife out of the drawer and laid it on the bed.

muscle—a tissue composed of fibers that contract to effect bodily movement, from the Latin *muscul*, little mouse—how tenderly the ex-schoolteacher helps her elderly mother eat, yet no kindness overrides the gossip you heard first. On the other hand, your first impression of anyone gets lost once you've touched, even lightly, nervous like a mouse, like your tongue in your mouth.

queue—a line of waiting people or vehicles, from the Old French *cue*, tail—and what about polyamory? You have your string of hearts albeit stretched out over time. And hasn't each preceding love, bright or faint, enriched the next? Is Pluto any less dear now that we know it's not a single planet but simply the largest of sixty-odd ice and rock cometlike objects?

solstice   ever rides

my highest goal, he answers, is Frances

(premonition)
          his face among that evening's sparked
a memory
                    no single weather repeats itself exactly

but the sun   as far north in the sky as it ever rides

     then   it's agreed

gist—the main idea; the essence, from the Old French *gésir*, to lie—it was watching him watching "Anal Sex #19" that stirred her, delighting in the idea of the whole thing, certainly not in those shaven pubes: the image of the wiley businessman reaming the maid, which still popped up weeks later. But isn't that always the way? One's pleasure lies in the other's.

sfumato—the blurring of lines, from the Italian *sfumare*, to fade out—and they meet again, after twenty years, at the bar out on the highway. One remembers the way the other would push his cowboy hat from his face with his beer. The world is stamped with tenses, every bird-beaded roadside existing equally, none caring about any other as a jet's roar fades into a dog's bark.

twist—to wind together so as to produce a single strand, from the Middle English *twisten*, a divided object—the shadow on her liver's still there, but "good news!" sings the doctor, her bones seem cancer-free. Husband cries with joy in that moment God's speed flies towards him; frozen to the track, he thinks: could this life (her in bed and two demanding children) go on for years?

susurrus—a soft rustling sound, from the Old Latin *susurrare*, to whisper—his daughters and second wife take turns bringing him dinner. "Only do what you want," he murmurs. The wrong analysis. All these years they'd lived apart, she loved him; now: paralysis. She has to laugh, left only with the rustle of hospital sheets as he uses his legs like flippers to change positions.

aver—to affirm positively; declare, from the Latin *ad + verus*, true—midnight: a windowful of mild moonlit air, he beholds his little boy's toy hat, wife's bald head. Her psychiatrist clearly confirmed the rage he'd witnessed for years. So did her sister; in her fifth month of chemo, appalled by this gang warfare, she declares them all dead wrong.

étui—a small, often decorative case for holding articles like needles or toiletries, from the Old French *estui*, prison— an incorrigible flirt, thick wavy hair and a new baseball cap: taking it off, putting it back on, he doesn't know what not to ask. "Where *is* France?" he asks a girl from there. The walnut shell imprisons the walnut: here, the reverse.

splendid   this way

obsessions really can't be

      sprung out of the jail of erratum then spun
splendid
      over her work, weaving, weaving
          on the path, one of a garland of planets

"You've got to take care of your temple,"
the yoga teacher said as she blew
      her hair dry

for years, the disciple never listened to music
nor picked a flower

the more you feminize, the more you want to—playing again
with the rosebuds of his nipples, his cock smiled

utopia—an ideally perfect place, from the Greek *ou,* no
+ *topos,* place—he wanted to talk to the dead; she preferred
surprises: his funky, black Fiat parked perfectly against a swarm
of purple sage. Anything his excited her sometimes; lying in
bed with her hand down his shorts, she finds it miraculous that
garbage trucks still cruise the streets in the rosy light of dawn.

interruptions   finally

good to be by another species

not so other—smooth variances:
she sweats only through the bottoms of her feet

after three years in Colorado, you're swept away to the mountains
                collecting rose hips and wild mushrooms...

        delightfully physicality fails to (be) matter
foremost what I want for you—him kindness like a stream

an entire gene pool restored with each blithe nip
flocks on the Western plains   as I walk room to room, crumple
                                a sheet of paper

crumpled sheets
                finally   flow   flower   us

elide—to omit in pronunciation, to strike out, from the
Latin *ex* + *laedere*, to wound—the older he gets, the less the
close-in interests him. He neglects to mention his hernia,
focusing instead on a news clip: the explosion of a star older
than the sun. The thought that the universe has always existed
excites him: "Something that is everything could never not be."

etymon—an earlier form of a word in the same or an ancestoral language, from the Greek *etumos*, true—the blue bill of Audubon's spoonbill, Doubting Thomas's hand reaching into Christ's wound: things stay with you, and you don't know why. Your friend's dog dies, and you sense it that very morning. Things happen, and you assign a meaning true to the past.

Easter   looking into

country in the moon

next door they've brought a foster baby home
to live in their lofty green house; he's looking into
another pair of eyes that's not quite right
baby's made from many-colored bundles
jocose as a nest of eggs

while tenderly leaves unfurl
we bomb what none of us have seen

green mansions   turned to

tall room of the living to see her out
      she wrote stories we turn to—
"The man on the bench, an out-of-towner exhausted from
finding his way…"
        —to find our way   said the mole-near-his-lip man
old postcards: rounds of apologies, raillery, hopes

gold beetle   upturned on the counter,

                        finally noted

her daughter, her Leonard   all lush   fictions for Gina

shambles—a scene or condition of complete ruin, from
the Middle English, *shamel*, a place where meat is butchered—
some things look so immovable, you can't imagine they'll ever
move again: like the orange truck parked every morning where
the blackberries thrive between Burger King's and Goodwill's
garbage. Then the gulls fly in and carry things away.

shape—the outline or form of an external surface, from the Old English *gesceap*, creation—the blue shining (a starship from across the field), a plastic window. From up here, bedrolls of fog, grey swatch, green swatch, my own street, my own roof, how the town got created the way it did. Living down there, I know it's not perfect, neither the world nor we are, the match is.

escape—to break loose from confinement, from the Latin *ex + cappa*, cloak—he once lived where they grew pineapple, a rough hut on the beach enough; he can't be sure he's the same man: it's easy leaving him behind, but not this man now. Out the door, there is the cloud-cloaked sky: gulls swept towards the sea like dice rolled across a table in a smoky room.

rescue—to set free from danger; save, from the Old French *rescuer, re + escourre,* to shake—an abstract of someone fishing, aptly painted in blues and greens, is set out of harm's way; we do so much to avoid disaster. But it's almost as if there's no life, no living without a canoe tipping over, heartbeats bobbing, and afterwards, the man telling the story has us all shook up.

tempering

•

brush against,   brush with death

birds bead the balcony
          dawn spires

countless stories of two kids   dropped like eggs into hot water

alseep in your bed, her long beauty
every man could love   so long

••

you boarded a ship
no land ho

mostly fate swims beyond character
here is pain's bandwidth, individual as

wasted   months of watching one life slip   away
about the time the purple sky

found:
a Linda
a pearl
rightawayrightawayrightaway

overboard

fall night: ringing from a night in jail   for naught
for not knowing how to leave/her bones into your bones
you stayed
            that's all—just as you stayed   unilluminated
                  opening hospital curtains   offering:

"Look! It's such a beautiful day."

•••

            reading her Buddhists, the obsessive loop loosens

it happens   each ordinary, like a softening stranger,
speaks in molecules
                        and the prior world seeps
slowly,

            a bowl   coconut milk soup

disarrangement   nosing closer

necrotic nectar for the maggots   poor dog's nose nosing closer

a late night tiny picture disclosing
                    the natural world neither with nor without
kindness
            like waves leaving/
                    not lyrics scrolled in the sand—

you there, rushing soap to me, rushing towels

                discard the sickle moon flavoring the sky

your body a just-struck cymbal, silvery leaf, sea-washed
shell
            be in me   occlude mortality's
                                        flatness

vent—a means of escape or release; an outlet, from the
Latin *ventus*, wind—being vulnerable re-pairs those who
like the inescapable bruising that comes of trying to escape.
A chill wind, still the pear tree's frills stick like snow, like stars
to sky, flies to fly paper. Whoosh: we stir each other up; stick.
Cooling off, finger-play in a pool of come, a little indoor ice
rink: swoosh.

thwart—to prevent the occurrence of, from the Middle English, *thwerten*, across—"no bras showing, no slouchy pants, no bare midriffs"; the twins, thirteen in November, discretely circumvent the school's new dress code. The one who walks with a crutch, has on a lovely, little spaghetti-strap tank; she's looking across an imaginary divide, which, of course, isn't imaginary at all.

fine—of superior quality or appearance, from the Latin *finis*, end—a stunning discovery: Jupiter-like planets traveling in elliptical orbits around seventeen extrasolar stars; which points to the rarity of nine jewels in circular orbits around a G star. How often we don't recognize the end of something (the last time you drive down a road) even in ourselves.

top—the highest or loftiest point or part of anything, from the Icelandic *toppr*, top, tuft—expectations flying off beyond the brassy tufts of native grass, clear to the mountain's hazy crown: no more word from the tower today than on any other day, not for the boy rounding up chickens nor the man freeing a squirrel from a trap. We think there is. There may be in other realms.

noise—a sound that is loud, unpleasant, or unexpected, from the Latin *nausea*, seasick—sawed into eighteen-inch logs, yesterday, the shaggy giant lay across the road. No one there had even heard the crash, but the fallen oak had pull, not unlike the moon making and unmaking the sea, passengers steadying themselves aboard a ship sailing to a country they've only heard about.

neuston—the minute organisms that inhabit the surface layer of a body of water, from the Greek *neustos*, swimming—though Kerouac dove into Buddhism, it seems he was equally immersed in the death of Christ. In his early journals (begun at 14), short prayers and thumbnails of crucifix abound: we marvel at such pearly minutiae then wonder whence the deep preoccupations arise, seemingly born before we are.

pining   requires

        every green chassis brushes a sunny dominance
dog ghosts the garden   merrily absence hosts presence

gesture upon gesture, sans discussion, the body of love rises
       splashing cool water   in the smooth chamber

    beneath the climbing vine, the mound of earth has settled
grief requires a body and someone looking back
       faraway whistling,   hips rusting

SMCL

3 5151 00226 3846

PHOTO: Eliot Holtzman

STEFANIE MARLIS grew up near
Buffalo, New York but has been living
in the San Francisco Bay Area since
1974. She has two previous full-length
collections: *rife*, which was published by Sarabande Books in
1998, and, *Slow Joy*, which won the 1989 Brittingham Prize
and was published by the University of Wisconsin. *Slow Joy*
also received the 1990 Great Lakes Colleges New Writers
Award selection. Marlis has received an NEA fellowship
and three California prizes: two Marin Arts Council Awards
and the Joseph Henry Jackson Award. Her poems have been
published in numerous journals, including *Arshile, Gettysburg
Review, Ploughshares, Volt,* and *ZYZZYVA.* For the last ten
years, she has been making a living as a freelance copywriter.
Marlis lives in San Anselmo, California, with her dog Sappho.